Free Pilgrim 2

— P I L G R I M —

 FriesenPress

Suite 300 - 990 Fort St
Victoria, BC, V8V 3K2
Canada

www.friesenpress.com

Copyright © 2018 by Pilgrim
First Edition — 2018

ISBN
978-1-5255-3041-8 (Hardcover)
978-1-5255-3042-5 (Paperback)
978-1-5255-3043-2 (eBook)

1. Travel

Distributed to the trade by The Ingram Book Company

Table of Contents

For my loving wife May "bersherte" and constant companion with whom I share the joy -

For my understanding children Selena and Nigel from their imperfect father-

For all the kind souls who decide to walk with me despite our differences -

Introduction

Free Pilgrim 2 is a sequel to my book *Free Pilgrim*, which is the story of my journey down physical, spiritual, and mystical paths. This second book is comprised of narratives from seven trips to different places and ancient sites on this planet, as I continue with my life-long journey. Life experience is no longer like "Buddha Jumps Over the Wall". To me, life experience is like the soup in a "Hot Post" as I go about gathering ingredients for this pot of soup through my wanderings and globetrotting. I retired many years ago from the professional life of a lawyer and a banker and decided to go on cultural and religious pilgrimage to ancient and sacred places around the world, with the intention of sharing my experience and perspectives with readers who are interested. It is my hope that readers who are unable to visit these fascinating destinations will be able to see and visit them vicariously through this book. It is also my hope that *Free Pilgrim 2* will continue to motivate others who are blessed with the opportunity to travel and who intend or have intended to make similar journeys. «Journey to Siberia and Beyond» is just one of the seven tales in this sequel, and its beginning.»

Journey to Siberia and beyond

INTRODUCTION

It is the month of May. Leaving allergic rhinitis aside, it is my favourite month of the year. It is in the middle of Spring, with the promise of a beautiful and lively Summer (perhaps even in Siberia). This month of May is especially special for me as we would be weaving along railway lines towards the "unknown"- to Siberia and beyond...

I have flown by planes, driven cars, sailed on cruise liners and traveled by trains (both fast and slow) for quite many years now. My favourite mode of transportation in this modern age and uncertain time is undoubtedly by train despite the fact that on occasions I had to sacrifice a bit of creature comfort. I was fully aware, in the process of planning for this journey by train, that we now live in unstable and dangerous times. It was all in the news in the Spring of 2016. In Brazil an economic and civil upheaval was happening before the Olympics. But more importantly the world is in despair with political instability almost everywhere. Brussels, Iran, North Korea, Paris, Syria, and the list goes on. So, I chose train travel if I could. There is less bureaucracy and the security check-in for train travel is relatively a breeze. Train (some with Wi-Fi on board) can also be considered a gadget paradise with electrical outlets fitted in cabins where one will not have to experience the frustration of a drained-out battery. Whether rain or shine, inclement weather or otherwise, the train runs. Looking out, looking in front, looking behind we have a vista of passing and ever-changing scenery and because the luggage is travelling with us or even besides us there is no need for us to look or even wait for them at the end of our journey.

When I mentioned to relatives and friends that I would soon be embarking on a journey by train from Moscow to Beijing I could sense that a picture would form in their minds of the romance of the "Orient Express". While "journey by train" from Russia to China conjures up a picture of romantic travel; the reverse, "transportation by train to Siberia" conjures up a picture of deportation, forced settlement, hard labour and death. There were many unfortunate events in human history concerning Siberia. However, I learned that some who had survived those Siberian tragedies had eventually lived out the rest of their lives bringing good to humanity. From these survivors (who could forgive and give) we need to draw our lessons. Little had I realized that this journey of mine would unexpectedly and ultimately also turned out to be a lesson for me as a "Journey of Forgiveness".

MOTIVATION

On the other side of Asia bordering Russian Siberia lies Northern China (what used to be known as Manchuria). It is officially known as the Northeast. Manchuria is separated from Russia largely by the Amur, Argun, and the Ussuri rivers; from North Korea by the Yalu and Tumen rivers, and from Mongolia by the Da Hinggan Mountains. The Manchu people formed the last imperial Qing dynasty of China (1644 – 1912). The 1800s of the Qin Dynasty is of special interests to me as a descendant of the Hong (Hakka Fung) clan who were involved in the Taiping Civil War. From 1850 to 1864 The "Taiping Rebellion" or "Taiping Civil War" was fought between the established Manchu-led Qing Dynasty and the Christian millenarian. The Taiping Rebellion began in southwestern province when local officials launched a campaign of persecution against a Christian sect led by Hong (Fung) Xiuquan who was a Hakka. The scholar of Chinese history Stephen Platt recounted these events in spellbinding detail in his book "Autumn in the Heavenly Kingdom". Until recent time what had happened had been labelled by the victors as a "rebellion". In his book (with in-depth research) Stephen Platt described it as a "Civil War" and framed his story about two (2) fascinating characters with opposing visions for the future of China. On the side of the Qing was Zeng Guofeng (a conservative Confucian scholar) who emerged as the most influential military strategist in China's modern history and Hong Rengan (Jen-Kan) a brilliant Taiping leader whose grand vision of building a modern, industrial, and pro-Western Chinese state ended in tragic failure. The irony was that the Western powers in the Taiping Civil War eventually sided with the Manchu-led Qing Dynasty and defeated the Taiping Heavenly Kingdom Movement of Hongs (Fungs). Hong Rengan was executed by the Qing authorities in Nanchang in Jiangxi on 23 November 1864.

The Qing authorities continued to commit unspeakable massacres against the Hakkas, executing at least 30,000 Hakkas each day during the height of their operation. Christian Hakka descendants of the Hong (Fung) clan and other Hakkas sought "self-exile" overseas. Some emigrated in order to escape the persecution by the Qing imperial forces which were seeking to exterminate all remnants of the Taiping Kingdom. So, my great grandfather emigrated with his wife and three children to Guyana aboard the *Dartmouth* which landed in Georgetown on 17 March 1879. After living there for a number of years in British Guyana they returned to China and eventually migrated to British North Borneo where my father and I were born.

History has shown us many lessons about the "Victors and the Vanquished" but we only choose to point to and remember events that have bearing on our lives. In recent time we use the term "Cultural Genocide" as if it were fashionable to do so. We pass judgement on matter of "Cultural Genocide" while sitting on the "bench" under the very "culture" introduced to us by those we accuse. To me apology and monetary compensation is not the way to appease those in the incident of so-called "Cultural Genocide". In addition, it is incumbent upon us (particularly for those of us who are Christians) to imbue and inspire forgiveness to the very people we are to render apology. Only through forgiveness one can find peace and freedom of the heart. "Forgiveness does not change the past, but it does enlarge the future"-Paul Boese. "When we forgive we are destroying barriers, we come closer to others"-Jean Vanier. "It is in pardoning that we are pardoned" – St Francis of Assisi.

Perhaps popular culture makes cowards of us all and leads us to finger-pointing at (and blaming) others and at history. I recall the thought I had as I was approaching the City of St. James towards the end of my pilgrimage to Santiago de Compostela ...In conformity with popular culture we "prefer to remember the ills of some but choose to inter the good of so many with their bones".

4

THE JOURNEY BEGINS...

Vladimir Lenin, following the success of the Russian Revolution, moved the capital of Russia from St. Petersburg to Moscow. Modern day Moscow has been capital and the cultural hub of Russia since March 5, 1918. It is the capital of a country spanning eleven-time zones, from St. Petersburg (Russia's "Window to the West") all the way to Vladivostok. There are three ways to travel by train from Moscow to Beijing: - Trans-Russian, Trans-Mongolian and Trans-Manchurian. With Manchuria in mind I decided we would take the Trans-Manchurian route. We flew into Moscow from Toronto Pierson International airport by Finnair via Helsinki. Having spent a night in Helsinki we arrived Moscow on the auspicious day of May 13th (refer to my blog "Solitude (Subiaco), Italy regarding significance of "13th").

Looking at Saint Basil's Cathedral on Red Square.

The Red Square. Historically the Square had been used occasionally as a site for the coronation of Russia's tsars. It has been used frequently since as a place for official ceremonies by all Russian governments.

The Kremlin wall by the Moscow River

A night view of the Bolshoi Theatre. The Theatre is a historic theatre designed (by architect Joseph Bove) to hold performances of ballet and opera.

Komsomolskaya Metro Statio

Anyone who is a traveler (and I don't mean just a tourist) and has spent considerable time overseas and internationally will understand and appreciate that travel, above everything else, builds bridges between nations, countries, religions, cultures, people and races.

It is not the purpose of this article to talk about the sights and sounds of Moscow which we did enjoy immensely. Suffice to mention here an incident that happened to us during our short stay in this urban sprawl. On the third day of our stay (having visited some of the more popular and famous landmarks in Moscow) we decided to walk to the Cathedral of Christ the Saviour. It was Sunday 15th May 2016. After having walked quite a distance we realized that we were lost. I then sat down on the steps of a local church and tried to locate our position on the city map which had been given to us by our hotel. Suddenly we witnessed a procession of some kind. To me it was a parade of humility. It reminded me of Micah 6:8 (KJV). This was Pentecost Sunday... *St. Paul also describes the reality of being a Christian disciple: "I have been crucified with Christ and I no longer live, but Christ lives in me. The life I live in the body, I live by faith in the Son of God, who loved me and gave himself for me"* (Galatians 2:20).

Russian Orthodox Pentecost Sunday procession

Earlier I had to quickly moved away from the steps of this church as the procession was approaching.

Events happen, and people come into our lives for a purpose. Events happened so that we may learn or draw experience from them for the common good. Some people come into our lives to show us the right path for the common good; some will lead us astray. I believe the paraclete (Holy Spirit) acts only for the common good. What is not for the common good is of the other spirit that has gone out into the world-1 John 4:1 (KJV) "Beloved, believe not every spirit, but try the spirits whether they are of God: because many false prophets are gone out into the world".

After "accidentally" witnessing the Pentecost procession we went (again) on our way to "SEEK" the Cathedral of Christ the Saviour. In the end we would "FIND" the Cathedral somehow with the help of three young Muscovites who were very eager to show us the way on this Pentecost Sunday. Perhaps bias media and politics had given me a wrong impression of a country and its people...

On the way to The Cathedral of Christ the Saviour

The Cathedral of Christ the Saviour

A happy wedding at the Cathedral of Christ the Saviour

I learned that the original Cathedral (consecrated in 1883) was demolished in the year 1931 under the espoused "state atheism" in that era. Reconstruction began after the fall of the Soviet Union and the present Cathedral was completed in 2000. Today on our visit to this Cathedral we saw a beautiful footbridge leading to it from Bachug across the river and on one side of the Cathedral stood the commemorative statues of Alexander II and Nicholas II. The Cathedral square is graced by chapels framed after the same design of the Cathedral. This was the venue for the canonization of the (last) Tsar Nicholas II and his family in the year 2000.

The Petrovsky Boulevard of Moscow

Some cultural dancers

A huge Selection on Barbecue Grills

Russian cheese cake

After having enjoyed the sights sounds and foods of this fascinating city we began our Trans-Siberian train journey—one of the greatest train journeys in the world

INTO THE UNKNOWN

I had already planned for quite sometime, even though with some trepidation, to cross by train, the enormous Asian continent encompassing two of the largest countries in the world. Russia, with its enormous land mass, at 17,075,200 square kilometres, is geographically the largest country on the globe; and China (currently) in population count is also the largest country in the world: http://www.worldometers.info/world-population/china-population/.

Our train from Moscow to Irkutsk

Security on the platform of the railway station

Chinese cabin attendants (from Moscow to Irkutsk) who related to us their experience across this frozen land in the middle of the severe Siberian winters.

Nobody, well may be a few or some, would want to go to Siberia. Many thinks of Siberia as an endless place with fields of ice as far as the eyes can see or they imagine a terrible exile there from which there is no return.

On 15th July 2016 at 11:30 pm we found ourselves at the Yaroslavsky station soon to begin embarkation on this journey into the "unknown". We waited at the Station for our train #04 to pull along side platform #1 for us. We boarded the train and entered our coach with high hope and much anticipation. These coaches (a bit dated) were lined with carpets (well patronized) and framed in wood effect paneling. The berths were covered with red silk seat covers (of another era). We had a compartment with two berths, a shared sink and shower between two adjoining cabins – there are doors which can be locked on both sides. The configuration of our cabin was a lower and an upper berth with a single seat on one side of a small table. Upon boarding we were provided with clean white towels, white bedsheets and white pillow cases. Our neighbour in the adjoining cabin was a Russian woman by the name of Yanna who had emigrated to New Zealand and was now living in that country. This was her trip back home to New Zealand after having visited her relatives in Moscow. Yanna turned out to be a much sought-after interpreter for Alexander (our random acquaintance) and us...

The corridor of our train from Moscow to Irkutsk

The configuration of our cabin was a lower and an upper berth with a single seat on one side of a small table. The berths were covered with red silk seat covers (of another era)

Upon boarding we were provided with clean white towels, white bed sheets and white pillow cases.

Alexander (our random acquaintance) with Yanna (our random interpreter)

With the compliment of Alexander our generous random acquaintance.

Separated by a cabin on the other side away from us was Alexander, an influential Russian economist and businessman (whom we eventually found out). To me he was influential enough to make phone calls to his contacts to bring him food and medicine at various train stops along the way. Alex, an amazing man with tremendous generosity, who did not speak much English would show us photos of his family and friends on his laptop computer. Intermittently, he would share with us the provisions brought onto the trains for him by his contacts. It is because of Alex that we had the opportunity to enjoy Russian "pizza" and fruits among other Russian home-style meals and savory ... In consequence thereof, we only had one meal a day in the dining car even though there was an excellent Chinese chef on board who had made me a great train breakfast of bacon and eggs (sunny side up).

My breakfast on the train from Moscow to Irkutsk.

Dining car of the train from Moscow to Irkutsk.

So, these strangers came into our lives. What was the purpose of it all? Perhaps to widen my horizon and to teach me and let me understand that not all Russians are like those demonized by some bias Western media. Alexander, Yanna, May and I would spend several days (trying to understand each other) enjoying each others company during those long train rides heading towards the very edge of Western Russia before crossing the Ural Mountains towards Siberia. On board our train were also 11 German scientists and veterinarians. We all admired (and some of us took photographs of) the vistas passing the seemingly unending tracks through the forests of Siberia as we headed deep into the very heart of Asia. Regrettably Alexander and Yanna were taking the express route to Beijing which meant they would not disembark with us at Irkutsk Siberia. So, we thanked them and bade adieu (late at night) as we would be disembarking at Irkutsk in the wee hour of the next morning.

Miles of unending tracks passing through Siberia

Locomotive of our train from Moscow to Irkutsk.

A remote village in Siberia The endless Siberian forests near the Altai region

Five days and with approximately 4199 kilometers (2609 miles) behind us our train wound its way into the city of Irkutsk. Irkutsk was founded in 1661 as a settlement for trading gold and furs but has grown into a city of about 600,000. The city proper lies on the bank of the Angara river. Today, it is home to several universities and a major branch of the Russian Academy of Sciences. It is a major stop for the Trans-Siberian Railway as it lies halfway between Moscow and the two eastern terminus cities of Beijing and Vladivostok. In the planning for this journey I did some research about Siberia as we would be going into the "unknown" (leaving the rest to faith and hope; much as we did during our pilgrimage on the Camino de Santiago). Although not very much is revealed to me by Google I had decided to make Irkutsk as a place to break our Trans-Siberian train journey for a few days and to spend some time to enjoy ourselves in the culture of this region.

Sunrise in Irkutsk seen from The Angara Hotel

Professional filming of some scenic spots of the city

Epiphany Cathedral (built in 1718–1746)

Inside a Russian Orthodox Churches in Irkutsk

As we strolled along the back street of this magnificent city we met a curious old lady who was eager to get to know us (only if we spoke the language).

Many of the wooden houses in Irkutsk adorned with hand-carved decorations had survived and stand today in contrast with the surrounding Soviet apartment blocks.

Another interesting old wooden house which has survived in the modern part of Irkutsk

On the way to The Church of St. Nicholas (under restoration) in Irkutsk

TO LAKE BAIKAL

Lake Baikal the largest and deepest fresh water lake in the world.

On the day after we arrived Irkutsk we decide to visit Lake Baikal (the largest and deepest fresh water lake in the world) which lie approximately 72 kilometers (45 miles) away from Irkutsk. It is believed that Baikal is the world's most ancient freshwater lake. Although more than 300 streams and rivers flow into Lake Baikal it has only one outlet, the Angara. We hired a car for 5 hours having in mind to spend about 3 hours at lake Baikal with an hour (each way) getting there. Georgy our driver (unlike some reckless ones we had encountered in Moscow) turned out to be very courteous to us and respectful of our needs

Georgy our very careful driver.

Hotel Baikal

We had three hours to spend at Baikal Lake. It was lunch time, so we decided to have lunch in one of the restaurants which special-ised in grilled Baikal fish. The fish coming right off the lake were really fresh. However, unlike sea water fish, fresh water fish tend to be a little more bony and bland because of the lack of salt in them. Georgy was waiting patiently for us in his car. By the time we returned to the car after lunch he had already had his sandwiches and was smoking his Russian cigarette. It took us a bit longer on our return trip because of the heavy traffic by the time we reached the out skirt of the city. We stayed one more day in Irkutsk and decided to visit the embankment and the local open market before departing for the next leg of our journey to Beijing.

May having a look at the special Baikal clay bread-maker oven and loaves

Strolling along the embankment by Angara River

The weather was beginning to change on our visit to the open market in Irkutsk.

Back to the market in Irkutsk before we boarded the train for the next leg of our journey heading for Beijing.

TO ZABAYKALSK... ONWARDS TO BEIJING

Our train from Irkutsk to Zabaykalsk onwards to Beijing

Lake Baikal as seen from our train on the way to Ulan Ude before it skirted along the Mongolian border heading eastward towards Manchuria (Northern China).

The Corridor in our train to Beijing – a passage way which enables us access to separate cabins or compartments

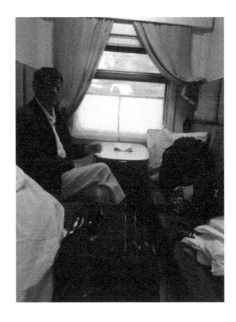

Our cabin on the train from Irkutsk to Beijing with convertible twin berths

Our cabin attendant checking on the boiler for hot water on the train from Irkutsk to Beijing.

Alexander, unbeknown to us, had already informed his contact in Zabaykalsk about us even before we arrived Irkutsk. His contact was the manager of one of his two duty-free shops at the Russian/Chinese borders. So, when we arrived Zabaykalsk, Tatania (Alexander's Manager) and Irena were at the platform of the station to greet and welcome us. Tatania, who was not conversant in English, was helped by Irena who had studied at Transbaikal State University. With the help of a driver (Victor) and comfortable van they took us to see many interesting places before treating us to a sumptuous lunch.

At City Park in Zabaykalsk with Tatania and Irena

Collecting pendants of St. Nicholas

Close-up of the trio as we went up the hill overlooking the Chinese border!

Tatania had brought us provisions for the trip from Zabaykalsk to Beijing while saying "Прощание (farewell)" to us. We were so grateful and felt blessed with the generosity and kindness of these complete strangers who had crossed path with us along our journey...

TO MANZHOULI

A distant view of the Chinese border from a hill on the outskirt of Zabaykalsk town Russia

Zabaykalsk, I am given to understand, has been a trans-shipment station for a "break of gauge" since the 1930s. Around that time the Russian Railway for the Chinese side was sold by the USSR to Manchukuo and converted from the 1,520 mm (4 ft 11 $^{27}/_{32}$ in) gauge of the Russian Railways to the 1,435 mm (4 ft 8 $^{1}/_{2}$ in) of the China Railways –

"One common method to avoid transshipment is to build cars to the smaller of the two systems' loading gauges with bogies that are easily removed and replaced, with other bogies at an interchange location on the border. This takes a few minutes per car but is quicker than transshipment *of goods. A more modern and sophisticated method is to have multi-gauge bogies whose wheels can be* moved inward and outward. *Normally they are locked in place, but special equipment at the border unlocks the wheels and pushes them inward or outward to the new gauge, relocking the wheels when done. This can be done as the train moves slowly over special equipment."* https://en.wikipedia.org/wiki/Zabaykalsk. I had no idea which method they used for our train because I was not able to see what they did. May and I, together with the travellers from Germany were told to wait inside the railway station in Manchukuo while works was being done on our train (which was running on different gauge width).

Border Crossing Russia/China

The Russian townlet of Zabaykalsk is situated across Manzhouli where we also spent a few hours to clear customs and immigration into China. I was now on Chinese soil. In ancient times the area was inhabited by many tribes that lived in Manchuria. I am given to understand that during the decline of China's last dynasty the house of Qing (1644–1912) ceded the outer Manchurian territory to Russia in the 1858 under the Treat of Anjun. Argun River which originates in this area effectively is now the border between the China and Russia. I had, in my teenage years, learned about the massacres against the Hakkas Hongs "Fungs" by the Manchurians in the aftermath of Taiping Civil War. To me, what had transpired in the past should now just remain a part of our history. We may not be able (or may be there is no need for us) to forget but we can or should be able to forgive. It is in our forgiveness that we are forgiven.

We arrived Manzhouli where we had to clear customs and immigration as we entered Chinese territory and jurisdiction.

By coincidence we met "Liew Li" an official at the Manzhouli Station check-point. "Liew" is the family name of my mother.

Leaving Manzhouli for Harbin China. Harbin is famous for its winter festivals.

Our train arrived Harbin Station.

Listening to interesting stories and enlightening our-
selves talking with fellow passengers.

We spent a full day (our last) on the train passing through the lands of mysteries, rice fields, vast factories in smoky and smoggy industrial cities (of this economic power house) onto the ancient Capital of The Middle Kingdom.

Wind turbines in the mystic land of rural China

We helped our cabin staff to clear our compartment and Saying "Goodbye" to Inna our "Host".

The price of progress. Vast factories in smoky and smoggy industrial cities

Beijing West Railway Station platform. Arrived Beijing West Railway Station

Chinese High-speed rail

As we had already been to Beijing on other occasions we decided to spend only two days in this progressive ancient city. From Beijing we would take the fast (high-speed) train south to Hangzhou to see Richard our neighbour (in Canada) who originally came from Hangzhou.

Just a thought:

In Hangzhou we would meet up with Richard from our old neighbourhood in Coquitlam British Columbia Canada. So unexpectedly Richard and Irene had somehow come into our lives in Canada. Richard, who was at the time in China when we arrived, picked us up from Hangzhou East train station. He spent three days with us showing us all the wonderful sights of this beautiful city and then drove us to the airport for our direct flight to Sabah... That is another story... but more importantly, who is your "neighbour"?

"But he, willing to justify himself, said unto Jesus, and who is my neighbour?" – Luke 10:29 (KJV).

Journey to Cyprus

Everything happens for a reason. I have been blessed with the opportunity to have had a long connection with the island of Cyprus. It has taken me quite sometime to understand...

Cyprus is the easternmost isle in the Mediterranean. It is situated at the crossroads of civilizations and has long been a place influenced both by the East and the West. Artifacts at the Cyprus Archaeological museum represent objects from the earliest villages to masterpieces of medieval religious arts. They provided me with an overview of the unique culture of this Land. The earliest known human activity on the island occurred when seafaring people from the Near East landed their boats there around 10,000 BC. Cities were first organized and built during the Ancient Near East Bronze Age. The island was part of the Hittite Empire during the late Bronze Age (Ref: "Cultural Pilgrimage") and the well-preserved Neolithic village of Khirokitia contain archaeological remains from this period. The island is home to some of the oldest water wells in the world.

Archeological finds on the island of Cyprus

Human remains, and artifacts found in Cyprus.

Bronze figurine of a "Horned God" from Enkomi, Cyprus. Enkomi is a village near Famagusta in Cyprus. It is the site of an important Bronze Age city, possibly the capital of Alasiya.

The Cyprus Museum (also known as the Cyprus Archaeological Museum) is the oldest and largest archaeological museum in Cyprus.

The Mycenaean arrived Cyprus during the last phase of the Bronze Age in Ancient Greece and since then the island has experienced an uninterrupted Greek presence. The Greek population of this Land survived through multiple foreign occupations, including Egyptian and Persian rules. Cyprus was conquered by Alexander the Great in the 4th century BC, and then ruled by the Ptolemaic Egypt until 58 BC, when it was incorporated into the Roman Empire. After Julius Caesar's assassination (March 15, 44 BC) Marc Antony and Octavian (later Augustus) struggled for power and control and in 40 BC Marc Antony gave Cyprus to Cleopatra (Queen of Egypt).

Mosaic at The House of Dionysus Paphos

Mosaics at The House of Theseus

The mosaics of the House of Theseus lie close to the House of Dionysus (dating back to the second century A.D.) where I observed the mythological representations and very interesting geometrical decorations.

From around 649 to 966 the island was under Islamic Caliphate and returned to Roman rule until the 12th century. In 1191 during the Third Crusade Richard I of England captured the island from Isaac Komnenos of Cyprus. He used it as a major supply base that was relatively safe from the Saracens. A year later Richard sold the island to the Knights Templar who, following a revolt, in turn sold it to Guy of Lusignan the King of Jerusalem 1186-1192. Guy of Lusignan, died in Nicosia in 1194. The descendants of the Lusignans continued to rule the Kingdom of Cyprus until 1474. In February 1489 it was seized by the Republic of Venice. Between September 1570 and August 1571, it was conquered by the Ottoman Empire, starting three centuries of Turkish rule over Cyprus.

Selimiye Mosque located in North Nicosia and historically known as Cathedral of Saint Sophia (a former Roman Catholic cathedral converted into a mosque). It is housed in the largest and oldest surviving Gothic church in Cyprus (interior dimensions: 66 X 21 m possibly built on the site of an earlier Byzantine church). It was sieged by the Ottoman in 1570, and following its conversion, the mosque became the property of the Sultan Selim Foundation.

Inside an Orthodox Church in Southern Nicosia

Inside a Salmiya Mosque in Northern Nicosia

In our time the island of Cyprus has been and is divided since the Turkish military invasion in the year 1974 (barely a year after the first of my many visits to this country). The northern one-third part is de facto under the administration of the self-declared Turkish Republic of Northern Cyprus even though according to international law the Cyprus Republic has de Jure sovereignty over the whole island of Cyprus, as well as its territorial sea and exclusive economic area.

Ledra Street Crossing Point at the time of my visit in 2014. After the Republic of Cyprus joined the EU it has become much easier to cross the border between the North and the South. The locals cross the Cyprus border daily do business or just to visit or shop at either half of Nicosia.

I am informed that among the many suggestions put forward to resolve the conflict, critical peace scholars suggested that a solution to the Cyprus conflict can only be found by including society on a broad base. It has been observed that political elites started to abuse the conflict as a source of power. Compounding the problem is ethnic origin. The Greek Cypriots see themselves as descendants of Plato and Aristotle whereas the Turkish Cypriots see themselves as descendants of the Ottoman rulers. Both communities also have different religious backgrounds and beliefs. At the time of this article the talks to secure Cyprus reunification enter "final stages". The Guardian reported: "A historic effort to end the division of Cyprus has begun in earnest as Greek and Turkish community leaders resumed reunification talks before a high stakes multilateral conference, the first since the island's partition 43 years ago. After 18 months of intensive negotiations to settle inter-ethnic divisions, Nicos Anastasiades and Mustafa Akıncı will attempt to finesse the details of a peace deal in Geneva this week by poring over maps and discussing territorial trade-offs before tackling the potentially explosive issue of security".

It is not the intention of this article to suggest political solution to the Cyprus conflict. As for myself, I believe that peaceful solution can only be achieved if there is "willingness" on both sides (ref: The Holy City: Understanding the Past). I believe all human conflicts are the result of our fallen nature and the "fruit" of the original sin of "pride"- false ego (ref: The Road to Ancient Corinth).

We can be assured that every event has a reason behind it. God is sovereign. There are not random chances. There are no out of control happenings. God's purpose may be hidden, and we cannot understand until we are guided by the paraclete. We are given the Freewill to choose, to have "willingness" to accept guidance by the paraclete. The story for now is that three years ago I packed my bag and, on this day, at this hour, I flew by British Airways via London to Larnaca Cyprus. This was supposed to be a trip to the island of Aphrodite to meet up with my daughter whom I have not seen for several years, but the trip also turned out (for me) to be a journey of discovery. It was a journey into the Acts of the Apostles; to follow the footsteps of Apostle Paul to the island of Cyprus

The statue of Aphrodite of Soli (the symbol of Cyprus) in the museum in Nicosia. Soli or Soloi (Greek: Σόλοι) is an ancient Greek city in the island of Cyprus, located southwest of Morphou. Soli dates to about the 6th century BC.

In the 1st century Cyprus was most noted for its copper and devotion to the goddess Aphrodite. I am given to understand, that though she is the Greek goddess of love (beauty, pleasure, and procreation) orgiastic ritual and ritual prostitution in her shrines and temples were also part and parcel of her cult. Perhaps the cult attracted Paul's attention. Paul (who was Saul of Tarsus) made his First Missionary Journey to Cyprus in the year around 45 AD. He landed at Salamis (a town on the eastern part of Cyprus near Famagusta) which I was blessed with the opportunity to visit before the Turkish Invasion in 1974. According to one legend Aphrodite was born from the foam of the sea. She floated in a shell on the waves and landed on Cyprus near Paphos. Every year people came from all over Mediterranean and the world to visit her temple on the site in the area of "Palaepaphos".

Visitors viewing the Aphrodite's Rock. It is located off the shore along the main road from Paphos to Limassol. The location, as the mythical birthplace of Aphrodite, makes it a popular tourist location.

CONVERSION OF SERGIUS PAULUS

After ministering at Salamis Paul journeyed from the eastern side of the island all the way to the town of Paphos on the west. According to tradition the conversions of the population to Christianity outraged the high priest resulting in Paul being ordered to be tied to a pillar and given 39 lashes. Perhaps these were the mentioned in Paul's letters to the Corinthians: "Five times I received from the Jews the forty lashes minus one. "- Corinthians 2 11:24

St. Paul's pillar Paphos

Ayia Kyriaki Chrysopolitissa Church was built around 1500 AD on the site of a small church which was destroyed in 59 AD by an earthquake.

Following the footsteps of St. Paul in Cyprus.

Paphos, at the time of Paul, was the seat of the Roman government in Cyprus. It was here that the Roman proconsul and Governor Sergius Paulus became a convert to Christianity. Sergius Paulus, upon hearing of the arrival of Paul and Barnabas (who was a native of Cyprus- Acts 4:36), sent for them. Accompanying the governor was a Jew named Elyma (also known as Bar-Jesus), a false prophet and magician who sought "to turn the proconsul away from the faith." Paul looked at him and spoke these words:" O full of all subtlety and all mischief, thou child of the devil, thou enemy of all righteousness, wilt thou not cease to pervert the right ways of the Lord? And now, behold, the hand of the Lord is upon thee, and thou shalt be blind, not seeing the sun for a season. And immediately there fell on him a mist and a darkness; and he went about seeking some to lead him by the hand. Then the deputy, when he saw what was done, believed, being astonished at the doctrine of the Lord."-Acts 13:10-12.

Apparently after having served three years as proconsul and governor in Cyprus, Sergius Paulus returned to Rome, where he was appointed to the office of Curator of the banks and channel of Tiber. Historical record on Sergius Paulus was recently discovered in Rome. "A boundary stone of Claudius mentioning Sergius was discovered in the city of Rome in 1887. It records the appointment (AD 47) of the Curators of the banks and the channel of the river Tiber, one of whom was Sergius. Since Paul's journey to Cyprus is usually dated to the first half of the 40s AD (and some scholars date his visit even earlier), it is thought Sergius may have first served three years as Proconsul at Cyprus, then returned to Rome, where he was appointed Curator. As he is not greeted in Paul's Epistle to the Romans, it is possible he had died before it was written" – https://en.wikipedia.org/wiki/Sergius_Paulus.

Although The Acts of The Apostles contains a mere nine verses about Paul's preaching in Cyprus which we often overlook (Acts 13: 5-13); this passage shed light on the first stage of Paul's missionary journey across Cyprus. Reading biblical texts with the help of archaeological evidence (from ancient "excavated" locations) and local traditions I believe these historical events had happened and in believing I am led to further understanding.

THE CHURCH OF ST. LAZARUS (AYIOS LAZAROS).

On this journey of mine I also had the opportunity to visit the Church of Saint Lazarus at Larnaca. The Church of Saint Lazarus (Ayios Lazaros) was built in the 9th century to house the reputed tomb of Lazarus, the man who was raised from the dead by Jesus. Reconstructed in the 17th century, the church is the most impressive sight in the town of Larnaca.

According to Greek Orthodox tradition, after Jesus raised Lazarus from the dead, the saint came to Cyprus and was later consecrated bishop of Kition by Paul and Barnabas. Lazarus' tomb was located here in Larnaca. Tradition says Lazarus' tomb was lost during the period of Arab rule (the Arabs made the first attack on the island under the leadership of Muawiyah I beginning in 649). His remains were rediscovered in 890, and briefly enshrined here before they were sent to Constantinople by Emperor Leo VI in 901. Notable icons I saw in the church include one of the Virgin and Child, one of St. George and the Dragon (1717) and a silver filigree icon of Raising of Lazarus (1659)

The Church of St. Lazarus (Agíou Lazárou) is a late-9th century church in Larnaca. It is an autocephalous Greek Orthodox Church.

The Church of St. Lazarus (Ayios Lazaros) has an open porch which bears traces of Greek, Latin and French inscriptions. From the porch there were steps which enabled me to descend into the evocative interior of the church.

Gothic arches of St. Lazarus Church.

The impressive interior consists of a central nave, two aisles and three domes which were boarded in at the time of my visit. Steps ascend to an elaborate 300-year-old Rococo pulpit.

From the central nave I could see the Iconostasis of the Church of St. Lazarus

A view of the Iconostasis from the left aisle of the church.

Underneath the church is the Crypt which contains Lazarus' empty sarcophagus...

Tradition says Lazarus' tomb was lost during the period of Arab rule (the Arabs made the first attack on the island under the leadership of Muawiyah I beginning in 649). The tomb was found in Larnaca in 890 bearing the inscription "Lazarus, four days dead, friend of Christ". Emperor Leo VI of Byzantium had Lazarus' remains transferred to Constantinople in 898.

On November 1972 during the renovations of the church some human remains were discovered in a marble sarcophagus under the altar and were identified as part of the saint's relics (apparently not all were removed to Constantinople in 898). These human remains have since been encased in a casket. Looking through the round glass opening on the top of this relatively recent casket I could see some human bones...Perhaps, like many of us at some point in our lives, I would "take the first step even if we don't see the whole staircase".

Just a thought:

Is it true that events happen for a reason? Perhaps we often fail to sense the guidance of the paraclete as events unfold in our lives. However, in retrospect (if we make the choice) we may be able (especially in times of hardship and tragedy) to discern and understand clearer. Is it true that because we are in a fallen world that we are all subject to illness? Do we believe and (therefore understand) that God is testing us and strengthening our faith in time of suffering? Are we being disciplined for our good so that we grow into the fullness of the stature of Christ and share in His holiness? Hebrews 12:7-13 (KJV).

I believe that there is the natural law of cause and effect which is also known as the law of sowing and reaping: "Be not deceived; God is not mocked: for whatsoever a man soweth, that shall he also reap. For he that soweth to his flesh shall of the flesh reap corruption; but he that soweth to the Spirit shall of the Spirit reap life everlasting"- Galatians 6:7-8 (KJV). Freewill is also given to us to make choices:" O that thou hadst hearkened to my commandments! then had thy peace been as a river, and thy righteousness as the waves of the sea" -Isaiah 48:18 (KJV).

Journey to Patmos

ISLAND OF PATMOS

By His grace we arrived safely on the island of Patmos in the year of our Lord 2016. Patmos is a small Greek island in the Aegean Sea measuring only about 12 km long and at its widest is 10 km from east to west.

It is situated at the northernmost of the Dodecanese, a group of some fifteen (15) larger and many other smaller Greek islands in the southeastern Aegean Sea near Turkey. Patmos is an important destination for Christian pilgrimage because it is associated with St. John's writing of the Book of Revelation. The Book of Revelation is the only book in the New Testament where the place of writing is given "I John, who also am your brother, and companion in tribulation, and in the kingdom and patience of Jesus Christ, was in the isle that is called Patmos, for the word of God, and for the testimony of Jesus Christ" -Revelation 1:9.

Skala Village is the centre of life on Patmos.

During my first journey to Ephesus in year 2009 I learned about the Basilica of St. John which is situated on the slopes of Ayasuluk Hill, Selcuk about 2.5 kms from Ephesus. Although not biblically mentioned I also learned then (from early church traditions) about John bringing Mary to Ephesus (Ref: "Steps of Paul") and his later exile to this island.

"When I heard that one of these [islands] close by Was Patmos, I wanted very much To put in there, to enter The dark sea-cave. For unlike Cyprus, rich with springs, Or any of the others, Patmos Isn't splendidly situated..." –Friedrich Holderlin's epic poem "Patmos".

Whether we think Patmos is "splendidly situated" or not, in our time thousands of visitors go to the island of Patmos every year. Many of them on pilgrimage. For the modern pilgrims there are many ways and forms of transportation to get to this island. We met a middle age couple from Ontario. The husband is a Greek man originally from the Greek island of Samos and the wife is a woman of Chinese heritage. They told us they sailed to Patmos from Samos by ferry. May and I were in Rhodes the previous day. As we sailed towards Patmos the first thing I noticed was the monastery of St. John crowning the hill of Chora like a Byzantine castle and a fortress. The weather condition was perfect and our small ship (unlike larger cruise ships which must anchor and tender) was able to be docked at the port of Skala. From the village of Skala we would take a coach up the hill to The Cave of Apocalypse (the Cave of St. John) and the Monastery of St. John.

As we approached the seaport of Skala (the Town of Patmos).

Patmos is important for Christian Pilgrimage. Today it is also the most visited place on the island because it is the island's only port. There are many hotels, restaurants, supermarkets, gift shops, bars, cafeterias and other amenities you would expect to find in a commercial harbour port.

The Monastery of St. John can be seen at a distance on the top of the hill.

Sometimes I ask myself why I go on pilgrimage; especially to sacred destinations. Perhaps there are many reasons – to feel the presence, to learn, to remember, to honour and above all to give thanks and to tell stories about them and share my journeys with those who care. Unlike the strenuous walk along the Camino de Santiago, the pilgrimage to Patmos does not take much time and is not particularly physically challenging. Before we started on this journey I had already read about the Cave of Apocalypse, this location and knew a little bit about life and legacy of the Saint...

BACKGROUND & MOTIVATION

St. John the Apostle Church Port Moody.

In the year 1996 while on sabbatical I attended services at St. John the Apostle Church in Port Moody. May had earlier been led to this small Anglican parish church not too far from our home in Coquitlam. Our son Nigel was baptised in this church. Although born and raised in the Lutheran tradition I learned that Orthodox and Catholic churches are often named after saints. I think it is nice to have congregation of a church under some sort of patronage. An Anglican priest once said to me that to him the name of a parish is important, and he does not take the name lightly. The name of our parish church has fascinated me ever since I joined the congregation of St. John the Apostle Church. I still do not know why our parish church (built in 1899) had chosen St. John as the patron saint. I decided to learn about this Apostle John who is also known as John the theologian and John the evangelist.

I learned that John was part of Jesus' "inner circle" along with Peter and James. John together with Peter and James witnessed Jesus' Transfiguration on mount Tabor -Matthew 17:1-9. The Apostle John (not to be confused with John the Baptist) is the brother of James (Ref: "Camino de Santiago") another of the twelve disciples of Jesus. The two brothers were called "Boanerges" (sons of thunder)-Mark 3:17 and from this we can find a key to John's personality. From scripture we come to understand that John, in his early days as a disciple of Jesus, sometimes acted quite boldly and impetuously -Luke 9:54. We read about him forbidding a man to cast out demons in Jesus' name because that man was not part of the twelve -Mark 9:38-41. However, by the time of crucifixion Jesus had enough confidence in John to place the care of Mary over to him. "Then saith he to the disciple, Behold thy mother! And from that hour that disciple took her unto his own home."- John 19:27.

The exterior of the surrounding buildings and the path leading to the entrance hall outside the Cave of Apocalypse (Cave of St. John).

A SMALL ENCOUNTER

During our journey to Patmos we met a friendly Indian couple from Melbourne, Australia. Perhaps they were supposed to come into our lives even for just a short while. The man, Felix (who introduced himself to me at breakfast) is a physicist. He is of Indian heritage, so he probably thought I was thinking he is Hindu. Pre-emptively he told me he is not Hindu but a Christian who came originally from Goa, India. I wanted to tell him that May and I had paid respect to St. Francis Xavier in The Basilica of Bom Jesus, but I preferred to listen to him. Felix told me he had spent 10 years in Saudi Arabia before immigrating to Australia with his family. He had worked in Saudi Arabia as an engineer setting up medical equipment in the government hospitals there. His specialty is in calibration. To me, his wife Alice is a devout Roman Catholic. She later related to us and shared with us her experience as she entered the Cave of St. John. She revealed to us that she somehow felled on her knees as she entered the Cave.

It was Sunday as we arrived the Cave (which is now also a Greek orthodox chapel) and a Sunday service was underway. A sign was displayed outside the Cave which stated, inter alia, no cameras video or photography were allowed inside the Holy Cave. I dutifully followed this instruction and stored my cameras inside my small backpack. As I entered the Cave I was...perhaps deep in thought... until I realized that an old woman (a member of the Greek Orthodox congregation) beckoned to me to go in front of the congregation to touch the rock which somehow, I managed to do. This was the rock believed to be where St. John slept on using it as a pillow. I also witnessed a devout middle age man making the sign of a cross and kissing it in veneration. I can only assume that the middle age man was Greek Orthodox. Seven silver lamps were hanging in the Cave. I have always known that each one of us has individual consciousness of the things around us and people are affected differently (if at all) when they visit places such as this. Christian traditions concerning such places point to a mystery which neither theologians nor the scientific community have yet been able to explain. Even though I did not fall on my knees (nothing physically happened to me in anyway, as much as I was aware) perhaps in other ways I also had a similar experience as Alice had...

Cameras allowed in the entrance hall to the Cave.

Gate to the entrance hall of the Cave of St. John.

The display charts in the entrance hall showing the setup of the buildings surrounding The Cave of St. Joh

THE MONASTERY OF ST. JOHN.

On top of the hill (not far from the Cave) is the Monastery of St. John constructed in 1088. This Monastery, with donation coming from the Byzantine emperors and countless private donations, is the richest in the Dodecanese. After the coach dropped us off we had to walk up a steep narrow paved road on the left of the road to Chora. We then passed a couple of restaurants and gift shops. At the end of the paved road, next to Artemis gift shop (where I bought a Visitor's Guide), we saw the stairs that lead to the Monastery. A man was in attendance in a kiosk to sell tickets and advised us that there are five chapels for us to visit.

As we entered the gate we immediately came across a courtyard laid with pebbles and cobblestones. There were graceful arches above me. I looked around and noticed many different levels to the Monastery. These were probably due to reconstructions, rearrangements and additions which have taken place over the centuries. In the centre of the courtyard I saw a round covered structure that looks like a well. On my left was the main chapel constructed in 1090. I turned and faced the main chapel (Katholikon) of the Monastery. There were four arched colonnades and behind the colonnades is the outer narthex with wall paintings painted centuries ago. Someone mentioned that the upper paintings were from the 17th century showing and representing different miracles performed by Saint John.

As I entered this magnificent Monastery I was mesmerized by the graceful archways and the paths and corridors paved with pebbles and cobblestones.

The arched colonnades outside the main chapel.

The paintings on the wall outside the narthex of the main chapel (Katholikon) of the Monastery.

Entrance to the main chapel (Katholikon).

One of the inter-connected staircases

There are several interconnected courtyards, arcades and stairways leading to five chapels. On the right, as we entered the Monastery, is a stairway going up to the old Treasury (where no photographs were allowed to be taken) and from there to the roof terraces.

The staircase leading to the old Treasury/ museum housing collections of chalices, crowns, vestments and rare icons.

On the way to the old Treasury/Museum.

The entrance to the old Treasury which is now also a museum.

From the museum we walked up a narrow staircase to the roof terraces to have a closer look at the church bells which we had noticed from the courtyard down below.

narrow staircase to the roof terraces.

A special moment with the church bells at the roof terrace.

The old treasury (which is now a museum) houses more than 13,000 manuscripts and volumes dating back to the Monastery's 1000 years history. I finally left this magnificent Monastery, caught the view of the Aegean from above, enlightened and enriched, as we made our way down to the sea port of Skala. I am thankful and feel blessed with the opportunity to visit these places...my journey would continue to the Meteora in Northern Greece...

View of Aegean from the Monastery of St. John

Just a thought:

Scholars of both critical and traditional orientation agree that John appeared to have been in some form of imposed exile on the island of Patmos (by the Roman Emperor Domitian 95 A.D and released by Emperor Nerva around 97 A.D). However, some modern biblical scholars believe that Authorship of the Johannine works (the Fourth Gospel, the three Epistles and the Book of Revelation) was not by the same author because of the style. I have the greatest respect for those biblical scholars. I do not know whether they are right or wrong. As for myself, I believe that even if the works were in different style as some modern biblical scholars think, that style can be moved or changed by the Holy Spirit. If we believe so, then we understand. If we do not believe, then we will not understand.

94

I believe John was the only one of the original twelve disciples not martyred. His brother James (St. James the Greater of Camino de Santiago) was the first to be singled out for martyrdom-Acts 12:1-2. After Jesus's Crucifixion John moved to Ephesus and took Mary with him. Perhaps for God's purpose he was exiled to Patmos and then back in Ephesus where he lived out the remainder of his life until 100 Anno Domini. I do believe he wrote the book of Revelation during a period when the Christian churches were experiencing persecution. I learned from John that even though he remained bold and courageous to his last days, his confidence was balanced by the humility he learned at Jesus' feet. Perhaps from this Apostle I have also learned never to have false pride gets in our way and to understand that there is a need for humility in those who desire to be great...

The life of John can serve as lessons. Zeal for truth should always be balanced by love for the people. Zeal can turn to harshness and judgementalism without love. On the contrary love can become just meaningless sentimentality when it lacks the ability to discern right from wrong, truth from error, good from evil. The virtue of confidence without humility can turn into evil pride (to be distinguished from "good ego"- see http://www.freepilgrim.com/the-road-to-corinth/). Witness of the grace of God is tainted.

The Meteora as seen from our hotel Famissi Eden.

Meteora

THE METEORA OF GREECE

We started our trip by car from Athens to the Meteora on November 1st, 2016. Nigel, our son, had flown in from Toronto to drive us to Northern Greece. We stayed overnight at the charming town of Arachova in order to explore old Delphi. From Delphi we proceeded to the Meteora situated near the town of Kalambaka.

Remain of the old Delphi as we see it in our time

We met a shepherd and his so special breed of sheep on the way to The Meteora.

It was almost evening as we were approaching the town of Kalambaka and from a distance the great Meteora came into our view.

The Meteora has been declared a world heritage by UNESCO. It is a formation of immense monolithic pillars and huge rounded boulders that dominate the area which was believed to have been built on the location of the ancient city of Aiginion. We had planned to spend some time around this location to explore the various existing monasteries. Second only in importance to Mount Athos the Meteora is associated with one of the largest and most precipitously built complexes of Eastern Orthodox monasteries in Greece.

Early morning view as we drove to the Meteora.

At their peak in the sixteenth century there were 24 monasteries at the Meteora. Most of these are perched on high cliffs which are now accessible by staircases cut into the rock formations. Only six of these monasteries are still functioning to serve monks and nuns who are following the teachings of the Eastern Orthodox Church. Currently, of the six functioning monasteries, the Holy Monastery of St. Stephen and the Holy Monastery of Roussanou are inhabited by nuns while the remainder four are inhabited by monks. At the time of our visit I was given to understand that the total monastic population of the Meteora monasteries was 66 with 41 nuns in the two mentioned above and 15 monks in other four.

The first monks appeared in this area at the beginning of the 11th century. But the monastery complex appeared to flourish only after the conquest of the Byzantine empire in 1453 by the Ottoman. Orthodox monks sought refuge in the remote locations at the Meteora because of persecution concern. The monks originally had to climb a series of ladders tied together or be dragged up there by a large net. Steps have since been carved into the rock and we were able to reach the Monasteries by foot.

The Hand-powered winch used for hoisting.

THE MONASTERIES

"The scenery of the Meteora and the ascetic life are two very similar things. Prayer, deep and wholehearted prayer needs something like the meteora. Something hard and imposing. It requires bare stone and sky. Lots of sky! "- Athanasios Kouros.

I believe that from early Christian times the vertical cliffs of the Meteora were probably regarded as the perfect site to achieve absolute isolation. To some it probably provided a perfect environment for deeper spiritual experience and the deepening of man's everlasting desire to connect and unite with the Divine.

The Monastery of The Holy Trinity

The Monastery of Holy Trinity (*Agia Triada*) is perched on a steep and magnificent rock. It is the most difficult to reach in term of distance as we had to follow a curving pathway that directed us initially to the foot of the rock before we would start walking up a straighter well-defined ascending concrete path and then another 150 steps or so. But once we were up there we had a breathtaking and panoramic view of the entire plain of Thessaly. This Monastery is very close to the Saint Stephen's Nunnery. As indicated in a document by *Symeon Uressis Palaeologos* it had already been an organized Monastery since the year 1362.

Distant view if the Monastery of The Holy Trinity

A closer view of the Monastery of The Holy Trinity.

The well-defined ascending concrete path that will finally lead to the 150 steps or so up to the Monastery.

Approximately half way up to the Monastery

The path to the Monastery of Holy Trinity.

Bridge to The Monastery of The Holy Trinity.

Constructed in the 15th century the katholikon (main cathedral) of the Monastery is dedicated to the Holy Trinity. It was decorated with frescoes in 1741 by two monks. The wall-paintings surviving today are the work of the hagiographers *Antonios* and his brother *Nikolaos*. Part of the Monastery served as the location and setting for the final scenes of James Bond movie "For Your Eyes Only".

The Monastery of St. Stephen (Agio Stefanos)

The Monastery of St. Stephen (Agio Stefanos) is located on the south west of Meteor at a height of 528 metres. According to an inscription, the origin of the monastery dated back to 1191/2 A.D. The official founder of the monastery was from the prominent Byzantine family by the name of Antonio Kantakouzenos. The main church, the Church of St. Charolabus, dates to the sixteenth century. The monastery was given over to nuns in 1961 and it is now a flourishing nunnery with more than twenty nuns in residence. We met several of the nuns during our visit to this monastery.

A distant view of the Monastery of St. Stephen

An easy entrance to the Monastery of St. Stephen

This is the most accessible monastery and certainly can be easily reached by foot. It is ideal for visitors who cannot use the steps and yet desire to have a real experience of a Meteora monastery. Instead of ascending steps we simply crossed a small bridge to reach the entrance where a nun was in attendance to sell tickets. During the time of our visit the cost of entry was only one and half euro each because it was off season. We understand the season lasts from April 1st to October 30th. The other two Monasteries were still charging three euros each. On the wall at the entrance there were shawls ready for women who were not suitably dressed or covered for entry into the monastery. Despite its easy access the site still provides incredible views of the mountains and the plain below.

The archway leading up to the Monastery

One of the large courtyards of the Monastery.

107

A relatively recent wall painting of the Sai

There are several large courtyard gardens and cloister areas where the nuns live. We found attractive souvenirs items innovatively displayed inside the gift shop. The whole place appeared to me beautifully land-scaped with tiny gardens perched precariously on the very edge of the rock. There were quite many visitors even though it was off season during the time of our visit to this Monastery.

The Monastery of St. Nicholas Anapafsas

The Holy Monastery of Saint Nicholas of Anapafsas (Agio Nikolaos) was supposed to be the first Monastery we had earlier intended to visit because I had learned that *Anapafsas* has to do with the monastery's position. It is situated at a location to be encountered first on the way up the Meteora. This Monastery probably served the pilgrims and other visitors as a resting place before continuing further up the Meteora. We were there on Friday November 4th. The Monastery was closed because it closed on Friday. We rescheduled our visit to the following day.

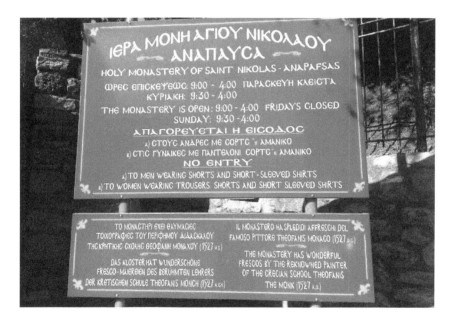

The sign showing opening days and time. Like all monasteries visitors must be suitably attired.

A distant view of the Monastery of St. Nicholas Anapafsas visible at the centre of this photograph

The St. Nicholas Monastery viewed from below.

Initial stage of the foot path up to the Monastery.

The Monastery at the first landing seen from the end of the foot path

The limited surface of the rock forced the building of the monastery to be vertically constructed one level on top of the other. The different floors are accessible through an inbuilt staircase. At the entrance of the Monastery lies the Chapel of St. Anthony. The chapel of St. Nicholas, which is the katholikon of the monastery, is on the second floor. The frescoes from the narthex of the Monastery's katholikon were painted in 1527.

The rock seen here is popularly used for climbing and from this location I saw climbers reaching the top of the boulder at the end of their climb.

The open terrace at the top of the Monastery.

The bell tower of the Monastery of St. Nicholas.

Amazing view of the valley below from another location on the top terrace of the monastery.

A small chapel in the grotto which provided space for prayer and meditation as one walks up to the Monastery of St Nicholas.

Chapel of St. Nicholas (the Katholikon) located on the second level of the Monastery

We visited all six of the monasteries but managed only to enter three of them i.e. the Monastery of the Holy Trinity, the Monastery of St. Stephen and the Monastery St. Nicholas Anapafsas particularly described above. The other remaining three of the functioning monasteries which we were able only to view from the outsides are listed below. I realized that in our time the monks and nuns are still trying (sometime under difficult circumstances) to preserve traditional orthodox monasticism to give us (who seek spiritual peace) guiding principles along our lifelong journey...

Dusk at The Monastery of the Great Meteoron.

Setting sun shining on The Monastery of Varlaam

Monastery of Rousanou viewed from the road below. We had walked up to this Monastery by a footpath and many steps (built on the side of this cliff) but due to time constraints we managed only to see its exterior and the surrounding area.

The following photographs will be without captions... People very often use words such as "serene, spiritual, magical, mystical, extraordinary, breathtaking, impressive" in an effort to describe the Meteora. Sometimes it is better just to let the photographs tell the stories themselves. Everyone looking at them will interpret according to their own individual imagination...

However, there is a little story of a lovely cat featured in two of these photographs that I like to share with those who care. While we were sitting on a roadside barrier admiring the distant view of the Monastery of St. Nicholas Anapafsas, a cat (which was probably from the Monastery of Rousanou nearby) jumped over the gap of the barrier, approached me and sat on my lap. I was wondering why a cat which I had never known before would do that. She lifted her head and we looked at each other in the eyes. She purred as she continued looking at me...Nigel said "Dad, the cat loves you". At that moment I was reminded of the time I had to talk to a crying donkey in a village near Villafranca del Bierzo while we were walking on the Camino (Ref: Camino de Santiago). Perhaps God has created some of them with the ability to see the third person in some of us. Although nowadays I no longer have a pet animal at home but years ago I used to have an adorable Japanese Spitz whom I named Rex. One day my Rex sneaked outside the fence of the backyard where we lived and was accidentally killed by a passing car. I gave him a "royal" burial on the slope of Signal Hill where we were in the process of building a new home...I have never had a pet dog ever since...

 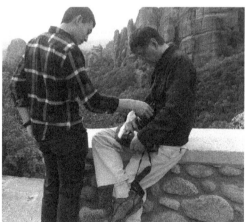

Just a thought:

The Meteora is truly inspiring with overwhelming rock formations. At the outset I thought I was just going on this trip for the purpose of enjoying an exquisite landscape, but it turned out that I really went for another. This turned out to be more of a journey than a trip. This was a pilgrimage to a sacred destination. This was a journey into a deeper understanding of God's wonderful creation.

I am thankful for the opportunity to be able to visit so many sacred places around the world. I realized that perhaps for centuries Christianity managed to flourish in part because of the large and impressive cathedrals and monasteries. In most countries with Christian heritage, strong buttresses and towering cathedrals and religious buildings dominated the landscape. One of the first things Christian settlers built in foreign lands were impressive churches, cathedrals and religious buildings. The same is even true in Canada, a country without an official state religion. Most of these magnificent cathedrals are still standing today but popular cultures put blame on the people who built them. In modern time we no longer enter monasteries, cathedrals or even churches just because they are there. To me, holy places were and are still important. They have served and can continue to serve to anchor communities in faith for the common good. Perhaps it is true that we, in conformity with popular secular culture, prefer to remember the ills of some but choose to have the good of so many interred with their bones...

Journey to South Africa and Beyond

Ancient Chinese Philosopher Lao Tzu wrote: "A journey of a thousand miles must begin with a single step." As a globetrotter I have encountered and experienced many cultures around the world and have come to realize that perhaps human is by nature inherently ethnocentric. We are all proud of our own culture and think ours is the greatest on earth. Is there a right or wrong or good or bad culture? In the Western culture, one of the most prevalent superstitions is the fear of the number 13. It is called triskaidekaphobia - (this word is Greek in origin: "Tris" is "3", "Kai" means "and", "deka" is "10", "phobos" means "fear")- The fear of the number "13". On April 13th, 2017 as a "free pilgrim" coming out of my comfort zone (and conquering triskaidekaphobia) I took a very uncomfortable flight from Vancouver via Frankfurt into Cape Town, South Africa with the hope of immersing myself in some of the cultures of the great African continent.

THE PERSPECTIVE

Several months before embarking on this trip I had already placed myself in proper geographical perspective. I have been informed that the standard Mercator Map does not reflect the true landmass of Africa. The world map was charted in the 1600s, according to the Mercator's projection. Despite being one of the most popular map projections (which I believe is even used by Google) the map makes Western nations appear larger than they are. In realty, the African continent can cover the total surface of the United States, China, India and the whole of Eastern Europe. As a Canadian I realize that Africa, geographically, is three times the size of our country. South Africa (as the name suggest) is situated at the southern tip of the continent and is divided into nine provinces. It has a coastline measuring in total about 2,798 kilometres in the Atlantic and the Indian oceans. By area South Africa is the twenty fifth largest country in the world. It is multi-ethnic with diverse cultures and languages.

For this Sojourn in South Africa I had rented a small apartment in Cape Town with a 24-hour Security, and access from both Adderley and Parliament street in Western Cape. Our host Christine, who is in the travel business, had earlier recommended to us many areas of interests, including the famous Table Mountain, Kirstenbosch, Boulder Beach and of course safari...

Table Mountain

Kirstenbosch

Boulder Beach

A lion in the bush.

But safari aside, Robben Island (declared a World Heritage Site in 1999) was really the centre and focus of my trip. The island acquired its name "Robben" from the Dutch "seal". At one time an abundance of seals populated the island. Robben Island served as a prison island and a place of banishment, and intermittently as an infirmary for almost three hundred years. An infirmary was established there in 1846 by the British Colonial Government. It was used as a medical institution (1846-1934) for three categories of sick people- those "insane", chronically ill and those with leprosy.

Mandela's Prison

Robben Island was used from 1961 by the South African government as prison for political prisoners and convicted criminals. In 1991 the government closed the maximum-security prison for political prisoners and the medium security prison for criminal prisoners was closed five years later. Nelson Mandela spent 18 of his 27 years of prison life on Robben Island. Mandela was prisoner number 46664 being the 466th prisoner to arrive in the year 1964. In his autobiography "The Long Walk to Freedom" he wrote: "In those early years, isolation became a habit. We were routinely charged for the smallest infractions and sentenced to isolation" and "I found solitary confinement the most forbidding aspect of prison life. There was no end and no beginning; there is only one's own mind, which can begin to play tricks." I learned that in the later part of his imprisonment he was housed in a cottage in a prison compound near Cape Town (known as Victor Verster) where he had TV, Newspapers, a swimming pool and was allowed visitors.

Prison Ground on Goree Island

The prison cell of
Nelson Mandela on
Robben Island

The window of Nelson Mandela's prison cell.

The burial ground on Robben Island

On 2 February 1990, FW de Klerk announced the ending of apartheid, the unbanning of the ANC (African National Congress) and the release of political prisoners which included Nelson Mandela. On Sunday, 11 February 1990 Nelson Mandela was released unconditionally from prison. To date, three of the former inmates of Robben Island i.e. Nelson Mandela, Kgalema Motlanthe and Jacob Zuma have gone on to become Presidents of South Africa.

With the end of apartheid, the island has become a popular destination with tourists from around the world. Thousands of visitors take the ferry from Cape Town for tours of the island and its former prison with tour guides (some of them were former prison inmates). Like many of these tourists in our time I could get a glimpse of this notorious Robben Island, situated not too far from Cape Town and the Table Mountain. I had the opportunity to meet an inmate and friend of Nelson Mandela who described to me the time and prison life spent on Robben Island. All land on the island (except for the Anglican Garrison church) is owned by the state of South Africa and managed by Robben Island Museum (RIM) which operates the site as a living museum...

Slavery and Oppression.

From South Africa I sailed to Cape Vert where in 1501 the Florentine navigator Amerigo Vespucci began to construct his "Mundus Novus" hypothesis about America: - Vespucci's letter from Bezequiche (1865) reproduced in F.A. de Varnhagen Amerigo Vespucci pp 78-82 (ref: Journey to the New World "Mundus Novus"). For me, this was a brief but purposeful visit to Dakar (the capital of Senegal) situated at the westernmost city of the Old World. I had learned that the area around Dakar was settled in the 15th century by the Portuguese. Goree island off the coast of Cape Vert and sheltered from the Atlantic by the Dakar peninsula was used as a base for the Atlantic Slave Trade.

Map of Slave Trade

Goree Island

Atlantic Slave Trade took place across the Atlantic Ocean from the 15th to the 19th centuries. I had the opportunity to visit the slave trade museum. I was "transported" back in time and within I was moved and felt the enormity of oppression and suffering which has long been forgotten. Goree has a notorious history as a slave depot. Today, on the island, I saw a cluster of pastel-coloured mansions and museums above the shore as its sleepy but perhaps scholarly present-day incarnation. The clear majority of those enslaved and transported to the New World were Africans from the western part of the African continent with some captured by slave traders in the coastal raids.

"The slave trade represents the biggest forced movement of people in history," says Elizabeth Khawajkie, the international coordinator of the UNESCO Associated Schools Project Network (ASP net) ...that is another story...

House of Slaves

But for the rest of us, the Whites or people from the West, in the present time, going to Africa and hugging poor children would do nothing to improve their lives, livelihood or the community even though it may make us feel good about ourselves.

Township (South Africa)

When accepting them as refugees into our country are we willing to welcome them into our own homes and encourage them to receive the Living Water? Are we not just being "alive" in this world but are spiritually dead if we are not willing to do so? Do we not "outwardly appear righteous unto men, but within are full of hypocrisy and iniquity". Would we not then be called "hypocrites" by gentle and loving Jesus? – Matthew 23:1-39 (KJV).

However, as for myself, I also believe the "coloured" and all those oppressed or who consider themselves oppressed (whether they are still in Africa or living in the Western world) should forgive the past and move on because we will always be in bondage and never be free until we have forgiven others for the wrong they've done against us. "The individual person is responsible for living his own life and for 'finding himself.' If he persists in shifting his responsibility to somebody else, he fails to find out the meaning of his own existence." ~ Thomas Merton

Freedom

Freedom (especially in the West) is considered the highest virtue. Freedom is sought after all by everyone especially by those who are (or consider themselves) oppressed. As I walked around Robben Island I could not help myself thinking about apartheid and slavery, the oppression and liberation of women, the Exodus story and the real meaning of "freedom". But in the biblical paradigm "freedom" is not social, political or economic freedom. "If the Son therefore shall make you free, ye shall be free indeed."-John 8:36

Some time ago I read that a Fr. Stephen of the Orthodox Christian Prison Ministry mentioned that over many years of being a prison chaplain he had heard this statement: "I am freer here in prison than I was ever on the outside!" How could that possibly be? How could someone experience more freedom inside a prison than on the outside?

Is South Africa free today? Perhaps there is social, political and economic freedom in South Africa. A BEE programme (Black Economic Empowerment) was implemented starting from 2003 which was later modified by the programme called Broad-based Black Economic Empowerment or B-BBEE. "It is an integrated and coherent socio-economic process. It is located within the context of the country's national transformation programme, namely the RDP. It is aimed at redressing the imbalances of the past by seeking to substantially and equitably transfer and confer the ownership, management and control of South Africa's financial and economic resources to the majority of its citizens. It seeks to ensure broader and meaningful participation in the economy by black people to achieve sustainable development and prosperity."

—*BEE Commission Report*

Despite modification the program is controversial in nature. Some consider its racial preference statements contradict the UN's Universal Declaration of Human Rights. At the time of my visit, South Africa was the only nation in the African continent where people are even free to marry members of the same sex. But as I observed during this Easter Season I could not help but got the feeling that despite this freedom, in this free South Africa, the people there are still in bondage. There is still chaos and tremendous discontentment within the society. Riots are common, and brawls even broke out more than once inside the Parliament itself. I came to realize that peace in this beautiful country may not come just through politics and economics. There is concern by some (with whom I discourse) that unless broad-based transformation happens spiritually post apartheid may also be the end of the coming together for the common good and the end of this "rainbow nation". The "myth of race" will always be there as in the rest of our world. Non-racialism is the rejection of the "myth of race". Multiculturalism is not non-racialism which is as distinct as night is from day.

Just a thought:

As for me, Exodus wasn't just a metaphor. I believe the story of Exodus repeats itself in every generation because there will always be people in bondage. "The thing that hath been, it is that which shall be; and that which is done is that which shall be done: and there is no new thing under the sun." - Ecclesiastes 1:9 (KJV). Exodus tells us that the Israelites (to whom God had given freedom) in less than 40 days after having pledged to keep the Law God had given them from Mt. Sinai, had already broken it...

It is instructive to remind ourselves that God has given us liberty not for the flesh: "For, brethren, ye have been called unto liberty; only use not liberty for an occasion to the flesh, but by love serve one another."- Galatians 5:13 (KJV)

*Our first cultural pilgrimage, with our son Nigel, to
Mesoamerica – Chichen Itza in 2008*

Journey to Mesoamerica

Life experience can no longer be like Buddha Jumps Over The Wall.
"...if any man think that he knoweth anything, he knoweth nothing
yet as he ought to know"-1 Corinthians 8:2. Life experience, for me,
is more like the soup in a Hot Pot as I go about purposefully collecting many different ingredients for this pot of soup through my
wanderings and globetrotting.

On the Feast Day of St. Margaret of Scotland in 2017 I left Vancouver
on my second cultural pilgrimage to Mesoamerica. This time to
ancient and colonial Nicaragua and Guatemala...to walk among the
ruins...with the hope of feeling the presence of the Aztec and Mayan
civilizations and a deeper understanding of their cultures.

Temple of the God of Wind and Castillo 2008

I had decided (on this second cultural pilgrimage to Mesoamerica) to visit specifically Nicaragua and Guatemala because to me these are two countries long forgotten by the West as we pondered over the United Nations Declaration on the Rights of Indigenous Peoples.

On May 28, 2015, in a speech, the then Chief Justice of Canada, Beverley McLachlin, referred to Canada's treatment of its aboriginal people as a "cultural genocide" that began in the colonial period. This term "cultural genocide" (frequently and "fashionably" used in Canada) was first conceived by lawyer Raphael Lemkin, who in 1944, distinguished "cultural genocide" or "cultural cleansing" as a component of genocide. Although juxtaposed with the term "ethnocide" in the 2007 United Nations Declaration on the Rights of Indigenous Peoples, the term "cultural genocide" was removed in the final document!

Two pertinent provisions of the Declaration are Article 7 and Article 8.

Article 7 1. Indigenous individuals have the rights to life, physical and mental integrity, liberty and security of person. 2. Indigenous peoples have the collective right to live in freedom, peace and security as distinct peoples and shall not be subjected to any act of genocide or any other act of violence, including forcibly removing children of the group to another group.

Article 8 1. Indigenous peoples and individuals have the right not to be subjected to forced assimilation or destruction of their culture. 2. States shall provide effective mechanisms for prevention of, and redress for: (a) Any action which has the aim or effect of depriving them of their integrity as distinct peoples, or of their cultural or ethnic identities; (b) Any action which has the aim or effect of dispossessing them of their lands, territories or resources; (c) Any form of forced pp transfer which has the aim or effect of violating or undermining any of their rights; (d) Any form of forced assimilation or integration; (e) Any propaganda designed to promote or incite racial or ethnic discrimination directed against them.

AZTEC AND MAYAN CIVILIZATIONS AND CULTURES

Civilization was probably born in Mesoamerica around 2500-1500 BC. The history of Mesoamerica saw the birth, the rise and fall of a series of cultures. However, much of Mesoamerican mythology and history was transmitted orally from generation to generation. Following more than a century of excavation we now know more about these civilizations; and yet still we know nothing for certain of events which had taken place more than 500 years before the Spanish conquest because of the Mesoamericans' willingness to blend fact with myth in historical accounts. However, the Spanish *Conquistadors* must also shoulder the major blame for the paucity of surviving remains as they vandalized and destroyed ancient images and artifacts. I am informed that even though three Mayan texts survived (and are held in European museums) most of the original writings were burned in the 16th-century.

Mesoamericans, not unlike our First Nations people, saw divine meaning threaded through nature and natural phenomenon. The Aztecs and Mayans worshipped a vast pantheon of Gods and Goddesses. An important central element of their civilizations was the use of human blood sacrifice to appease and propitiate their Gods. Classic-period inscriptions in ruins and texts suggest that both the Aztecs and Mayans were hungry for live prisoners; common folks were earmarked as slaves and the nobles were destined for human sacrifice. War was understood to be a natural condition and military conflict was a sacrament Victims were tied to sacrificial stones or posts and were slashed until their blood flowed freely onto the stones or the earth. They killed to preserve their culture and imposed theirs on others.

I was shown this sacrificial stone used in ritual blood sacrifice. Classic-period inscriptions in ruins and texts suggest that both the Aztecs and Mayans were hungry for live prisoners and rival nobles were earmarked for human sacrifice.

The years 250 AD – 900 AD (the classic period) represent the full flowering of their civilizations. Archeological finds and surviving documents provided intriguing insights into their development of mathematics and arts. They used a writing system that combined logograms and phonetic symbols. They also used a 365-day calendar based on sun movement and believed in a cyclical nature of time and in three planes: Earth, underworld and heaven above. But their history also reveals their grim commitment to wars and savage human sacrifice. Their civilizations were built around corn cultivation. Corn was not only an economic generator but also a sacred crop. However, as I had my meals during my visits in these countries, I noticed that rice and beans have taken over corn as the staples in their diets.

Although recently constructed this shows a writing system that combined logograms and phonetic symbols used by the Mayans.

NICARAGUA

The last time the world paid any attention to Nicaragua the country was mired in a decade-long civil war which began when the Sandinistas overthrew dictator Anastasio Somoza. Backed by the Reagan administration in the United States, the counter-revolutionary forces known as the Contras fought the Sandinista regime led by president Daniel Ortega. The conflict came to a peaceful end with the result of the election in 1990. The Sandinistas were defeated by the UNO coalition, led by Violeta Barrios de Chamorro.

On my birthday in 2017, I arrived Corinto, a town on the northwest Pacific coast of Nicaragua. This municipality was founded in 1863 but it was not the focus of my visit to Nicaragua. What had earlier prompted me to visit this country was the colonial city of Leon Viejo founded in 1524 by the Spanish Conquistadors. The city of Leon Viejo sits next to beautiful Lake Xolotlan and the active Momotombo Volcano.

From the hill above where the old fort is buried, I took in the fabulous view of Lake Xolotlan and the Momotombo volcano.

Volcanic activity in the year 1610 destroyed the original town and buried it in ash. It became known as the "Pompeii of Central America". In consequence of the massive eruption the population relocated approximately 20 miles west and established what is now known as the city of León. The ruins of the old city of León Viejo were hidden for more than four hundred years and was only discovered recently in 1967. It is now designated as a UNESCO World Heritage Site. On this journey I decided to explore these ruins with the hope of getting a sense of the early history of this first ancient capital of Nicaragua. I could have googled and read about much of these, but I also recall someone once said: "I hear I forget, I see I remember, I do I understand".

The site displays the 1524-1610 ruins of a city buried by ash and my imagination got a little carried away walking around architectural digs such as these.

This UNESCO archaeological site – one of the oldest Spanish colonial settlements in the New World, provided me an idea of its original layout and a glimpse into its past.

There were not many visitors on the site when I was there. For a UNESCO site I found it relatively and unusually quiet. As I walked around these ruins I could, periodically, hear the singing coming from the Guardabarrancos – the spectacular Turquoise-browed national birds of Nicaragua.

Leaving behind the ruins of this colonial city of León Viejo I proceeded to the present-day Leon, which in reality is not modern and new, but is rather a repository of Spanish colonial architectures with the pinnacles of churches soaring towards the heaven.

153

The Leon Cathedral

The altar of the Leon Cathedral

The Cathedral of León is the largest cathedral in central America. It is an important and historic landmark in Nicaragua. I decided to climb to the rooftop of this Cathedral.

Although it is the largest Cathedral in Central America the climb was relatively easy for me compared with what I experienced climbing up the Cupola of St. Peter's Basilica in the Vatican and the winding narrow staircase of St Paul's Cathedral in London.

View from the top of the Cupola of St. Peter's Basilic Vatican 2007

*View from the top of St. Paul's Cathedral London 200**7***

View from the top of Leon Cathedral.

157

But as I respectfully walked on the rooftop of this magnificent Cathedral (with my shoes taken off at the last stage of the climb) I was able to also get in an unmatched view of the "colonial Spanish" city of Leon below.

The domes on the rooftop of Leon Cathedral

Shoes were removed at the top of the Cathedral

GUATEMALA

As a Canadian I often imagine Guatemala to be just another tropical country. However, it is not necessarily tropical because of the terrains. The terrains of this country give it varying and different climatic conditions. My Spring jacket came out for the first time as I travelled up the highlands to an elevation of 2,260 metres (7,410 ft) above sea level.

Guatemala is also a colourful country, but the colourful materials worn by the Guatemalans are not signs of prosperity. The World Bank classifies Guatemala as a "lower-middle-income" developing country. The Guatemalans have an amazing culture, but their social and cultural growth was probably affected by the arrival of the Spanish conquerors. Today, their music comprises many styles and expressions. From 1524 on, Guatemala was one of the first in the New World to be introduced to European music. Many composers from the Renaissance, baroque, classical, romantic, and contemporary music styles have contributed works of all genres

Among the ancient sites I visited, I spent more of my time at Iximche which was the capital of the Kaqchikel Maya from 1470 until 1524. When Spanish conquistador Pedro de Alvarado arrived in 1524 (after the conquest of the Aztecs), he found the highland Maya kingdoms weakened by twenty years of internal warfare and the spread of the European plagues. In the period of February to March 1524 he fought and completely defeated the Kaqchikel Maya and executed the K'iche' kings. At the time of the Spanish Conquest Iximche was the second most important city in the Guatemalan Highlands.

On this journey I learned that the Mayans practised a cosmological sort of spirituality prior to the arrival of the Spanish. Temples were often aligned with the cardinal directions and arranged specifically to mark events like the summer and winter solstice. Caves were regarded as sacred passages to the underworld. As I toured the ancient city and it's ruins I was also able to witness and observe, from a distance, an authentic Maya ritual.

By observing this modern Maya religious ritual, I was beginning to gain a little insight into the rites often depicted in ancient Maya art.

The Mayan calendar is still being used in some places today, especially within the Western Highlands. This calendar is closely linked to the agricultural cycle, especially corns, which is considered a sacred crop. Corn is believed to have been involved with the formation of man by the gods as told in the *Popol Vuh*, a K'iche' book of mythos-historical narratives. The *Popol Vuh* includes the myth of creation, epic tales, and genealogies.

Temples at Iximche were often aligned with the cardinal directions and arranged specifically to mark events like the summer and winter solstice.

Temple 2 (the best preserved of the excavated temples) is a tiered pyramidal platform on the west side of Plaza A. It has a stairway on the east side of the structure, providing access from the plaza. It faces the sunrise on the summer solstice. Like many buildings at Iximche this Temple was also built in three phases. With the help of Lidar technology Researchers recently have found more than 60,000 hidden Maya ruins in Guatemala in a major archaeological breakthrough. Sprawling Maya networks were discovered under Guatemala jungle. Ithaca College archaeologist Thomas Garrison believed the scale and population density has been "grossly underestimated and could in fact be three or four times greater than previously thought". The Archaeologists believe that Lidar technology will change the way the world will see the Maya civilisation. "I think this is one of the greatest advances in over 150 years of Maya archaeology," said Stephen Houston, Professor of Archaeology and Anthropology at Brown University.

For the present traditional religious beliefs and practices of the Mayans continue to persist through the process of inculturation. Certain cultural practices are incorporated into Christian worship and ceremonies when they are sympathetic to the traditions. Indigenous practices continue to increase because of the cultural protections established under the Peace Accords. The government has instituted a policy to facilitate traditional ceremonies by providing altars at every Maya ruin.

Indigenous practices continue to increase because of the cultural protections established under the Peace Accords.

The Peace Accords brought genuine achievements but mixed with some serious limitations. The first breakthrough important achievement was the Human Rights Accord, signed in March 1994. It was important not so much for any new concept of human rights because these rights had already been guaranteed on paper in the 1985 Constitution. It appears to me that external as well as endogenous factors continue to influence the development of their cultural system. The processes are complex and the factors affecting their development were probably due, to a certain extent, to the relations between human groups and between humans and the environment. Regrettably, gender-based violence and femicide are still many problems in Guatemala. I read from the 2015 United Nations report that two women were killed in Guatemala every single day and according to Guatemala's national forensic investigations body, 222 women have been the victims of violent killings in the first four months of 2016 alone.

Evangelical Christianity has recently made an inroad into Guatemala. About one third of Guatemalans now are Evangelical Christians.

Catholicism was introduced to Guatemala during Spanish colonial times. It continues to have an important role in the community even though there have been some tensions (not unlike in Canada) between the church and other human groups. Evangelical Christianity has recently made an inroad into Guatemala. About one third of Guatemalans now are Evangelical Christians. The rise of Evangelical Christianity in Guatemala began in 1975, when earthquakes destroyed several villages in the highlands. International aid agencies, many of them Christians, rushed in to help and ended up converting the population to Christianity. Another factor that contributed to the rise of Evangelical Christianity was the civil war of the 1980s. I was informed that during this terrible time many Guatemalans found hope in a belief system that promised rewards in heaven despite an untenable situation in the present, in their worldly existence.

It has already been brought to my attention that some of the Guatemalan villages have almost been entirely converted to Christianity with incredible results. It is said that alcoholism, which was widespread in the town of Almolonga, is now almost entirely gone...

Just a thought:

Coming out of my comfort zone (like a frog jumping out of the well) I tried very hard to understand what really is this component of genocide called "cultural genocide" in the context of human existence and in the process of inculturation throughout human history? As a pilgrim, walking humbly (with God's help) I believe I can learn to understand who I really am in Christ. Perhaps understanding who I am in Christ would help me to realize that we, as Christians, should not really be the same as (or follow) the rest in and of the secular world. I believe that unless I can understand what makes me different *from* the world, I will not be able to make any difference *in* the world!

I am reminded of the following verse: " Thus saith the Lord God of Israel, Your fathers dwelt on the other side of the flood in old time, even Terah, the father of Abraham, and the father of Nachor: and they served other gods.[3] And I took your father Abraham from the other side of the flood, and led him throughout all the land of Canaan, and multiplied his seed, and gave him Isaac.[4] And I gave unto Isaac Jacob and Esau: and I gave unto Esau mount Seir, to possess it; but Jacob and his children went down into Egypt. " – *Joshua 24:2-3 (KJV).*

Journey Back In Time

JOURNEY BACK IN TIME

In this busy time, not many (even among family and friends) are interested in another's life story let alone read an autobiography or memoir. However, the main reason I love to globe-trot the world is because I find tremendous joy when people I meet are willing to share their life experiences with me. These are they, with different perspectives on the joy and pain of living, coming from different culture, social standings, stations in life and faith backgrounds. For some reason (perhaps for a purpose) they come and cross path with me along this my lifelong journey. My opening line to them: "Where is home?" The ice is broken... We would be engaged for some time after that opener...

Most I met, who are elderly with global exposure and experience, have lived interesting lives. Still, many have told me that they had wished they could go back to the good old days. I confess that I too have similar wish. Perhaps we are those who have chosen to remember only happy events within our lifetime. But there are others whose lives have been completely marred by abuse, hardship, betrayal, tragedy and pain and even by events beyond their lifetime: the time of slavery, civil wars and genocide. As a descendant of the Fungs (Hongs), I realize that the Qing Empire had probably committed what some would call "cultural genocide" on the Christian Hakkas in China! I have not forgotten but have forgiven the Qing forces for the massacre and persecution of the Fung Clan (which also created diaspora of the Hakkas) by the end of the Taiping Civil War (ref: Journey to Siberia and Beyond). Regrettably, within our popular culture, some historical incidents are being used to cause divisions, hatred, unrest and violence. Historical events should be judged in the context of its time. In the present, we are all personally responsible for our own lives. This short summary probably oversimplifies. Thomas Merton puts it succinctly : "The individual person is responsible for living his own life and for 'finding himself'. If he persists in shifting his responsibility to somebody else, he fails to find out the meaning of his own existence."

Like many, I also had a wish to revisit the past but we are constrained by the practical difficulties of journeying back in time! Perhaps I can, in spirit. That was exactly what happened to me in the month of September 2017 when I took a trip back to my Alma Mater, The Honourable Society of the Inner Temple in London, England. It is often said that a picture speaks a thousand words, but if one ever goes down to my Alma Mater one will quickly notice that it is even more magnificent seen in real life– and indeed even haunting – than a picture could ever present it.

The Temple Church under renovation in 2007

For me, this trip also turned out to be a pilgrimage to the awe-inspiring Temple Church. My last visit to this Temple site was more than 10 years ago. During that visit, with our son Nigel in the summer of 2007, the Temple Church was going under maintenance and closed. I was unable to show him its evocative interior.

I first set foot on the Temple ground in the Autumn of 1963, travelling as a law student from Shepherd's Bush where I had my lodging, to Chancery Lane Station (the nearest station to the Temple) on the Central Line. On this visit I decided to retrace my steps down memory lane. From the Chancery Lane Station, I walked along Chancery Lane passing the same shop from where I got my Barrister wig and gown more than 50 years ago. Then I crossed over Fleet St and enter the North Gate into the Temple ground.

Chancery Lane Station on the Central Line is the closest tube station to the Temple traveling from the north. From the South it is the Temple station on the District and Circle line.

Ede & Ravenscroft on Chancery Lane est. in 1689, (from where I got my Barrister wig and gown) has over 300 years' experience of specialist legal wear tailoring and wig making.

The Temple North Gate by Fleet street (the street once frequented by journalists. It remains popular and a metonym for the British national press

THE TEMPLE CHURCH

The Temple Church sits in between the Middle and Inner Temple, two of the four Inns of Courts in an area that evokes for me an overwhelming feeling of nostalgia. It is set against the backdrop of the Temple Garden. It was constructed by the Knights Templar, an Order (of crusading monks) founded in the 12th century to protect pilgrims on their way to and from Jerusalem. After the abolition of the Order in 1312, lawyers at the Temple site eventually formed themselves into two societies, the Inner Temple and Middle Temple, which were first mentioned by name in a manuscript yearbook of 1388. Historical record shows that since 1608 The Temple has been the collegiate Church of the legal colleges of Inner and Middle Temple. It stands at the heart of this unforgettably beautiful and historic part of London.

The Church is in two parts: The Round and the Chancel. It was designed (during the time of the Crusades) to recall the circular Church of the Holy Sepulchre in Jerusalem. The Round Church was consecrated in 1185 by the patriarch of Jerusalem.

View of the Round Church as we approached from the North Gate
The Round and the Chancel of the Church.

The evocative interior of the Church as viewed from the chancel

174

The Chancel as viewed from the Round

For many centuries, it has been the custom for Members of the Inner Temple to sit on the south side of the Church. For me, the Temple Church still exudes a strange energy of a place left encompassed by tales surrounding the awe-inspiring institution (now perhaps struggling to stand the test of time).

Here I am, as member of the Inner Temple, sitting on the South side of the Church where I first sat more than 50 years ago.

The Temple Church came to the public's attention several years ago where a scene was filmed inside the Temple Church based on Dan Brown's novel The Da Vinci Code. It is here that the main characters Langston and Sophie, along with Leah Teabing, tried to solve the riddle: "In London lies a knight a Pope interred. His labour's fruit a Holy wrath incurred. You seek the orb that out be on his tomb. It speaks of Rosy flesh and seeded womb".

The hero of Magna Carta was William Marshal, 1st Earl of Pembroke. Self-restraint and compromise was the keynote of his policy. He was a signatory as one of the witnessing barons to the Great Charter and was invested into the order of the Knight Templar on his deathbed. He died on 14th May 1219 and was interred in The Temple Church where his tomb can still be seen today.

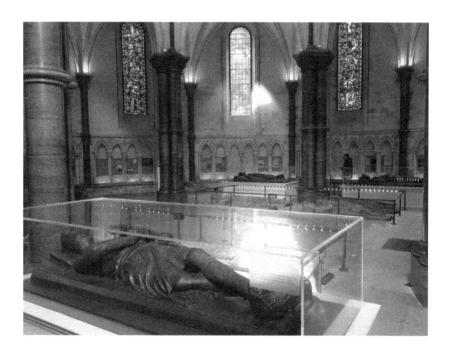

THE HONOURABLE SOCIETY
OF THE INNER TEMPLE

The Inner Temple was a distinct society from at least 1388, although as with all the Inns of Court the precise date of its founding is not known. The Temple has been closely linked to Magna Carta and its legacy ever since 1214. "The Temple was King John's London headquarters (1214-15). From here he issued two vital preliminary charters, and here in January 1215 the barons confronted him for the first time with the demand that he subject himself to the rule of a charter."- Robin Griffith-Jones, D'Litt, The Reverend and Valiant Master of the Temple.

The Temple has also been linked with the United States of America ever since. The lawyers from The Temple drew up the constitutions for the early American colonies. Five members of The Temple signed the Declaration of Independence, seven the American Constitution. The Magna Carta (or Great Charter) informs the legal system in Canada, and the Canadian Charter of Rights and Freedom. The agreement between King John of England and his barons provided the foundation for the English common law, which spread throughout the English-speaking world. I was delighted during our visit to witness the celebration of the Magna Carta and its legacy here at the Temple. During our visit we saw a special Magna Carta Exhibition in the Round Church and a few days after that I also saw an original copy of the Magna Carta at Salisbury Cathedral.

The Inner Temple and Magna Carta.

The Temple and the Declaration of Independence 1776

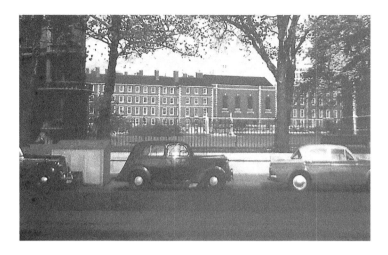

The Temple and the Temple Garden as viewed from the Victoria Embankment in 1964

In the essay "The Old Benchers of The Inner Temple" (published as Essay of Elia in 1823), Charles Lamb eloquently put it: "Those bricky towers, The which on Themme's brode aged back do ride. Where now the studious lawyers have their bowers; There whilom wont the Templer Knights to bide, Till they decayed thro' pride." ...

Reading for the Bar at The Temple Garden in 1964

Different times, different perspectives

THE TEMPLE GARDEN

The entrance to the Temple Garden in 2017

Shakespeare used the Temple Garden as a setting for the meeting between Richard Plantagenet and John Beaufort which sparked the Wars of the Roses, a series of civil wars for control of the throne of England fought between supporters of two rival branches of the House of Lancaster (red rose) and the House of York (whose symbol was a White rose). Some of these events of the wars were dramatized by Shakespeare.

Fountain and part of the Temple Garden in 2017

The present day lay-out of the garden has evolved not only over the last fifty years since I was there as a law student but over the centuries as the water in the Thames was controlled and the land claimed for building construction. Under the direction of Joseph Bazalgette, the construction of the Victoria Embankment started in 1865 and was completed in 1870. After the construction direct access from the Temple Garden to the river was lost. The Garden was completely re-shaped into a three-acre garden (that remains the skeleton design of today) populated with a rare and unusual collection of plants, flowers, shrubs and trees.

CONNECTION WITH THE TEMPLE

After completing Senior Cambridge GCE with Grade A (Division 1) I taught for two years as a temporary teacher in Lok Yuk School (a Basel Mission school) in British North Borneo. While I was teaching in this school my priest at the Mission tried to persuade me to enter seminary. But each of us is called for His purpose. By that time, I had already enrolled myself onto the University of London External Program for Law and simultaneously had also applied for admission to read law at one of the world's prestigious law institutions -The Inns of Court in London, England. The news finally came that I had been accepted for admission by The Honourable Society of the Inner Temple. I immediately made preparation to begin reading law in Michaelmas Term 1963. I remember vividly going into The Temple Church for the first time. The words of my priest (about going to seminary) still lingered in my mind as I found myself sitting on a pew in this unfamiliar place that seemed yet so familiar to me. This eventually was a place that I (as a young stranger in a foreign country) would find solace, peace, confidence and strength to carry on the monumental task of becoming a Barrister-at-law. The Temple Church was my refuge throughout the years of my education in England: - "Turn thee unto me, and have mercy upon me; for I am desolate and afflicted" Psalm 25:16 (KJV).

Dating back to 1506 The Inner Temple Library is a legal reference library. It sup-ports the information and research requirements of barristers, students and judicial members of all the four Inns of courts

I spent a considerable amount of time at the Inner Temple Library which had collections of books and law reports covering the legal systems of the British Isles, the Channel Islands, the Isle of Man, the Republic of Ireland and Commonwealth countries. I also found in the Library non-law collections which covered subjects such as history, biography, heraldry (mainly vexillology) and topography. There were also many other old books and manuscripts. A student by the name of Malek Ahmad was a regular at the Library. We came to know each other and became good friends. In later years we continued to meet up, from time to time, whenever I was in Kuala Lumpur At the Temple, some staff and some other students were also good company. We all learned to relax and enjoy our breaks at the Temple Garden, a haven of tranquility and beauty

. ...

With friends–different seasons, different times...

My friend Malek Ahmad with his black overcoat

Malek running for our photo-op.

Malek Ahmad eventually became President of the Court of Appeal in Malaysia. He died young in 2008. "He was the chief justice that the country should have, but never had". In the glowing tribute at the memorial service for (Tan Sri) Abdul Malek Ahmad, retired Court of Appeal judge K.C. Vohrah said: "The late Abdul Malek was an uncommon Malaysian, whose most important characteristic was his natural and tremendous sense of fair play and his unquestioned integrity."

THE GOOD THE BAD AND THE CHOICE...

Upon my arrival in England in the early days as a student, I was accommodated for one week under the aegis of the British Council. During that time, I met Mr. Longfield, a student adviser of the British Council who had an office at Oxford Circus. He explained to me that beyond this period of one **week**, the onus was upon me to have my own lodging. I was desperately looking for "digs" (within my monthly budget of 40 Sterling Pounds). I noticed a small advertisement in the Evening Standard regarding a room for rent by student. In answer to this ad I went to knock on the door. An elderly blond English woman opened the door, looked at me and said: "We don't take in Chinese" whereupon she closed the door. It was a classical case of "BAD discrimination". That was in the Autumn of 1963. A knife pierced through the heart a young man who had just left his home in Borneo for the first time in his simple life. He couldn't understand. "Turn thee unto me, and have mercy upon me; for I am desolate and afflicted"- Psalm 25:16 (KJV).

In the interim the British Council was able to recommend me an attic room at Old Oak Road, Shepherd's Bush where I would stay for an academic year before moving to Clonmel Road at Parsons Green to share a flat with a wonderful couple from Singapore. I revisited Old Oak Road with May and our son Nigel in 2007 and realized that someone with means had recently purchased the place and the building was under renovation at the time of our visit:

My attic room at Old Oak Road Shepherd's Bush

On the other end of the "spectrum" in the English society was a family who would invite me yearly to spend two weeks over Christmas with them in their lovely home at Highgate, North London. Everything had happened for a reason. It happened that on my way to England I was sailing in the old P & O Ship "Chitral" with 4 young VSO (Volunteering Service Overseas) from England.

Dining on board "Chitral" from Singapore to London

One of them was Peter Doulton (sitting next to me in the photo) who has remained a friend of mine for more than 50 years. Peter was returning to his home in England after his service as a teacher in rural Keningau, British North Borneo. He had left home for more than a year and his parent came to receive him at the dock in the Port of Tilbury London. Upon our arrival at the dock Peter introduced me to them and they immediately invited me to have lunch with them at their home the following Sunday. From then on, they would invite me to stay as their guest for two weeks over Christmas during my entire time as a law student in England. This couple had made me felt belong. Peter's father Mr. Doulton was the headmaster of Highgate School. He eventually retired to Salcombe, a resort town in the district of Devon, England. Peter wrote to me that when his father died, the parish church was overflowed at his memorial service...

Mr. Doulton with Peter's younger brother Roger preparing the table for Christmas at their home.

I have not forgotten but I had long ago forgiven that woman who had turned me away. I have always wondered what would have been if she had chosen to give us the opportunity to see the "third person" in each other. I have realized that the greatest tragedy in humanity is not the infliction of wrongs but the unwillingness and inability of man to forgive. Only through forgiveness one can find peace and freedom of the heart. "Forgiveness does not change the past, but it does enlarge the future"-Paul Boese. "It is in pardoning that we are pardoned"-St. Francis of Assisi.

Life has changed a lot in England over the years and I have witnessed the changes during my periodical visits to the Old Country. Change is being exerted upon us by secular culture and the politic of "political correctness". We now live in a fake and very superfluous culture of "Non-discrimination" in the world of political correctness. In certain respect "non-discrimination" is good but at the same time we have lost our God-given ability to discriminate (GOOD discrimination) what is right from wrong, truth from falsehood, good from evil. Man has always been tricked and pulled by the other force, but we are given the ability ("gift") and the freewill to choose. God has given us a brain to discern and a heart to love. It is our baptismal vow to love our neighbours and respect their dignity but not the evils manifested in human. Jesus love everyone but when he saw what was happening in the temple he did what he did... "And when he had made a scourge of small cords, he drove them all out of the temple, and the sheep, and the oxen; and poured out the changers' money and overthrew the tables" John 2:13–16 (KJV).

Our laws and values are based on biblical principles and Christian values. We have forgotten the blessings of the Judeo-Christian heritage. As our western societies continue to become increasingly secular, moral values inevitably erode to the detriment of everyone who lives in these countries. "Righteousness exalts a nation, but sin is a reproach to any people," – Proverbs: 14-34. Any society that condones destructive, sinful behavior (as defined by Scripture) is a society that will weaken and decline. Any change must be for the common good. We ought to have "a disposition to preserve" with an "ability to improve"-Edmund Burke. "Prove all things; hold fast that which is good."-1 Thessalonians 5:21 (KJV).

Just a thought:

"If the foundations be destroyed, what can the righteous do? Psalm 11:3 (KJV). To me, Conservatives and Liberals are probably similar, and we can walk together. Liberals look for change but Conservatives ensure that Liberals move progressively in the right direction. We do not throw the baby out with the bath water... We do have a choice...

We are told about evolution (or change as I observe myself in the photos "different times different perspectives") but TRUTH does not evolve (change). It is constant. The Son of God, the incarnate Word, the Word is Truth. "For I am the Lord, I change not; therefore, ye sons of Jacob are not consumed."-Malachi 3:6 (KJV). Since God does not change, the LIFE of our spirit is not at the mercy of changing events. In the natural world there are constants as well. There are fundamental physical constants (in physics) like the speed of light and the permeability of free space. There are mathematical constants, like pi and *e* which cannot change. I read somewhere in a science journal that even the structure of atoms is always going to be the same, isotopes notwithstanding. There is also Newton's law of universal gravitation and Einstein's theory of general relativity and so on...